CANADA NATIONAL SOCCER TEAMS

DAVID STABLER

Lerner Publications ◆ Minneapolis

Lerner Publications Company
An imprint of Lerner Publishing Group, Inc.
241 First Avenue North
Minneapolis, MN 55401 USA

For reading levels and more information, look up this title at www.lernerbooks.com.

Main body text set in Aptifer Slab LT Pro.
Typeface provided by Linotype AG.

Editor: Matt Doeden **Designer:** Viet Chu **Photo Editor:** Cynthia Zemlicka

Library of Congress Cataloging-in-Publication Data

Names: Stabler, David author
Title: Canada national soccer teams : ultimate fan guide / David Stabler.
Other titles: Ultimate fan guide
Description: Minneapolis : Lerner Publications, [2026] | Series: Lerner Sports. World Cup fan guides | Includes bibliographical references and index. | Audience: Ages 7–11 | Audience: Grades 4–6 | Summary: "The Canadian National Team is a growing force in the world of soccer. It boasts talented women, skilled men, and a passionate fanbase. Readers will discover the history and greatest moments of this team"— Provided by publisher.
Identifiers: LCCN 2025015754 (print) | LCCN 2025015755 (ebook) | ISBN 9798765689349 lib. bdg. | ISBN 9798348029265 pbk | ISBN 9798765698464 epub
Subjects: LCSH: World Cup (Soccer) | Soccer teams—Canada—History—Juvenile literature | Olympics—History—Juvenile literature | LCGFT: Literature.
Classification: LCC GV943.6.C5363 S73 2026 (print) | LCC GV943.6.C5363 (ebook) | DDC 796.334/660971—dc23/eng/20250626

LC record available at https://lccn.loc.gov/2025015754
LC ebook record available at https://lccn.loc.gov/2025015755

Manufactured in the United States of America
1-1012732-54802-7/30/2025

TABLE OF CONTENTS

Members of the Canadian women's national team pose before a match at the Olympics in 2021.

INTRODUCTION

OLYMPIC GOLD

Yokohama Stadium in Tokyo, Japan, was at the center of the soccer world in 2021. Fans across the globe watched as Canada's women's national soccer team stood on the brink of history. After years of hard work, they had made it to the gold medal match at the Summer Olympics. One final challenge remained—Sweden, a powerhouse team hungry for victory.

The match was fierce from the start. Sweden struck first to make the score 1–0. In the second half, Canada earned a penalty kick. Midfielder Jessie Fleming stepped up. She took a deep breath and fired the ball into the net. The game was tied.

As the clock ticked down, neither team could break the deadlock. Extra time came and went. It would all come down to a penalty kick shoot-out.

One by one, players stepped up. Canada's goalkeeper, Stephanie Labbé, made two incredible saves. Then it was Canada midfielder Julia Grosso's turn to take a shot. With a gold medal on the line, she ran up and struck the ball hard. It soared past the Swedish goalkeeper. Goal!

FAST FACTS

Canada's men's national soccer team will cohost the 2026 World Cup with the United States and Mexico.

In 1885, the Canadian men's team won its first international match. They beat the United States 1–0.

Canada's women's team first competed in the Women's World Cup in 1995.

The Northern Super League, Canada's women's pro soccer league, launched in 2025.

Jessie Fleming approaches the ball for a penalty kick in Canada's victory over Sweden at the Olympics in 2021.

The stadium erupted. Canada's players screamed, cheered, and collapsed in joy. They were Olympic champions! It was a great moment for the team as they brought home Canada's first gold medal in women's soccer.

Canada's men's and women's national soccer teams represent their country in the World Cup, Olympics, CONCACAF Gold Cup, and more. Both teams are filled with the best players from around the country. Fans flock to their matches to proudly display their national pride and love of soccer.

Canada's players and coaches celebrate the game-winning goal at the Olympics in 2021.

Canada and France battle in the 1986 Men's World Cup.

CHAPTER 1

RISE OF THE NORTH

Ice hockey is the national sport of Canada. But soccer also has a long history there. It took many years of hard work for Canada to become a strong soccer nation.

British immigrants introduced Canada to soccer in the 1800s. The nation's first major soccer match came in 1876 when the Toronto Football Club faced the Hamilton

Football Club. In 1885, the men's national team played its first match against the United States. Canada won 1–0. In 1912, the Canadian Soccer Association (CSA) formed. The CSA made rules and helped organize leagues for teams to play in.

Canada's national team poses in 1888, just three years after its first match.

For many years, Canada's men's team struggled to compete with the best teams in the world. But in 1986, Canada qualified for the World Cup for the first time. Even though they did not win any games, it was a huge moment for Canadian soccer. It showed that Canada belonged with the other great teams from around the world.

Canadian goalkeeper Tino Lettieri stops a shot at the 1986 World Cup.

GOLD STRIKE

In 1904, a Canadian men's club team won the gold medal at the Summer Olympics. No Canadian men's soccer team has won Olympic gold since.

Since then, Canada's men's team has worked hard to improve. After many years of missing the World Cup, they finally qualified again in 2022. With more young stars and better training, Canada hopes to become a top team in the future.

Canadian players Steven Vitoria (*middle*) and Atiba Hutchinson (*right*) gain control of the ball in a 2022 World Cup match with Morocco.

In the 1980s, Canada started a women's national soccer program. But women's soccer did not get as much attention as men's soccer. Players had to fight to be noticed by fans.

Over the years, Canada's women's team became stronger. They soon had more global success than the men's team. They played in their first Women's World Cup in 1995 and kept improving. In 2012, they won a bronze medal at the Olympics.

Midfielder Diana Matheson (*center*) evades a French defender at the 2012 Olympic Games.

Canada players show off their gold medals after the 2021 Olympics.

Then, in 2021, Canada's women's team made history. They won the Olympic gold medal, beating Sweden in the final game. It was one of the biggest soccer victories in Canada's history.

Soccer in Canada is bigger than ever. The women's team is among the best in the world, while the men's team looks to build on recent success.

Canada's men's team beat Mexico in the game known as "Iceteca" on November 16, 2021.

CHAPTER 2

CANADA'S FINEST

Canadian soccer has had many exciting moments. Both the men's and women's teams have made history. They've impressed their fans with big wins and amazing plays.

One of the most famous games happened on a freezing night in November 2021. Canada's men's team played against Mexico in Edmonton, Alberta, during a World Cup qualifying match. Snow covered the field. Fans bundled up in the stands to cheer on their team. The game became known as the "Iceteca," a twist on Mexico City's famous Azteca Stadium.

Canada defender Sam Adekugbe (*right*) tries to shut down Mexico's Jorge Sanchez in the Iceteca game.

Canada shocked the world by winning 2–1. It was the first time they had beaten Mexico in 21 years. After the match, the players celebrated by diving into snowbanks. This victory helped Canada qualify for the 2022 World Cup, their first appearance in 36 years.

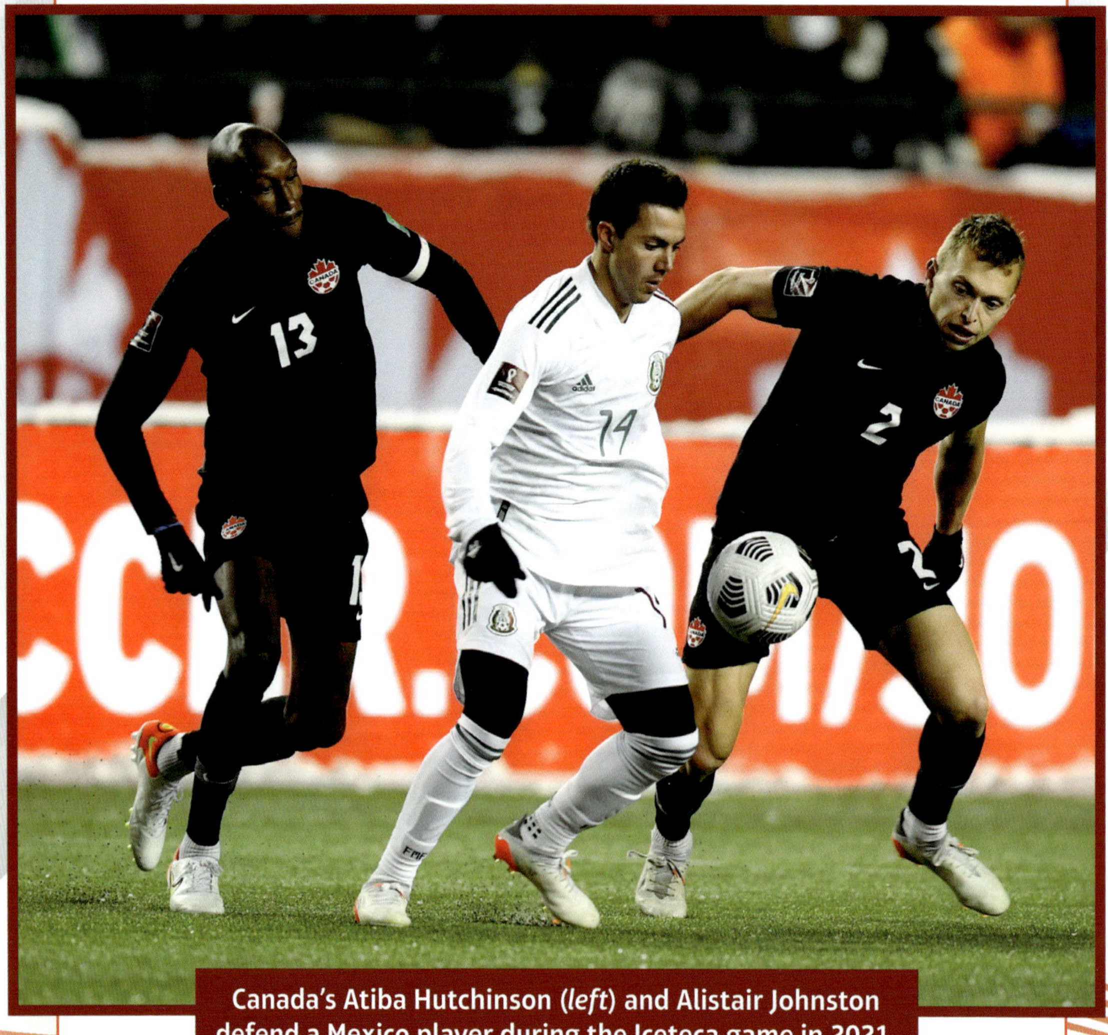

Canada's Atiba Hutchinson (*left*) and Alistair Johnston defend a Mexico player during the Iceteca game in 2021.

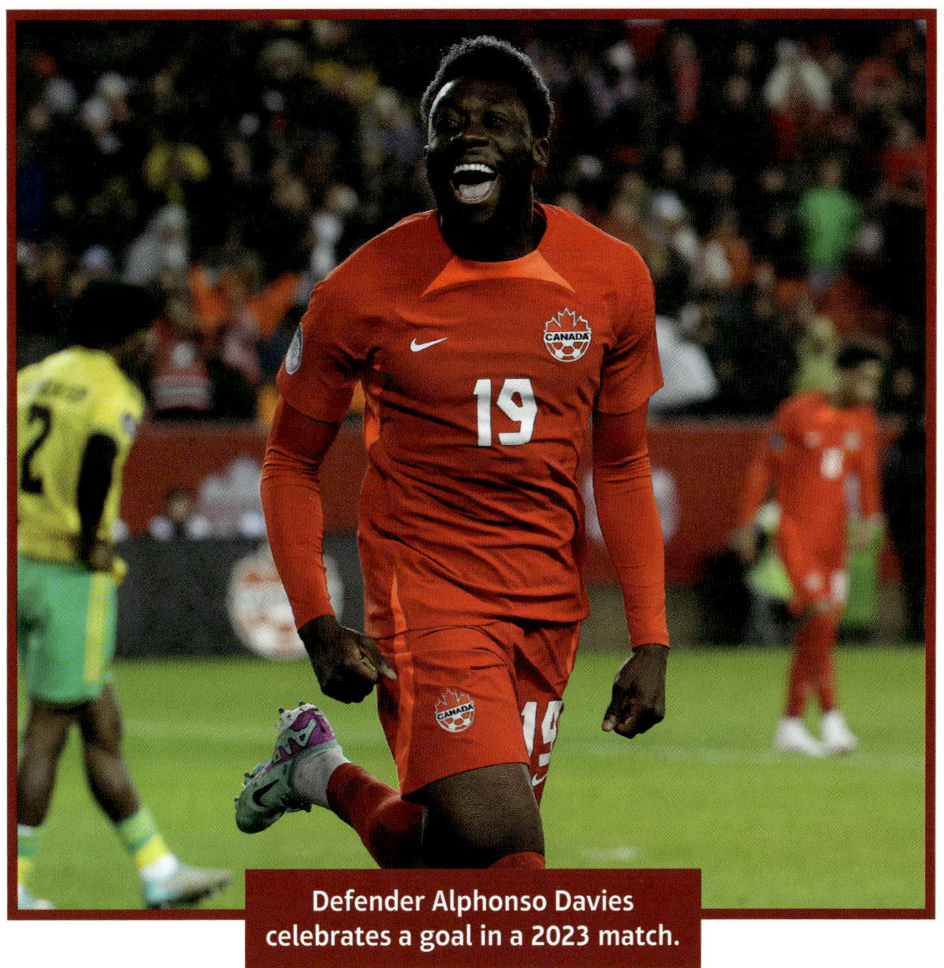

Defender Alphonso Davies celebrates a goal in a 2023 match.

One of the players celebrating in the snow that day was Alphonso Davies—one of the best men's players Canada has ever had. Born in a refugee camp in Ghana, Davies moved to Canada as a child and quickly became a soccer star. With his speed and skill, Davies helped Canada reach the 2022 World Cup and remains a force on the team.

Another star on the men's team is Jonathan David. With 32 goals and counting, David is the all-time leading scorer for the Canadian men's national team. He was named Canada Soccer Player of the Year in 2019 and 2024.

The Canadian women have also enjoyed many highlights. In 2012, they beat France to earn bronze at the Olympics. That was the first time Canada had won a medal in a team sport at the Summer Olympics since 1936. They won another bronze medal at the next Olympics in 2016, then finally captured the gold in 2021.

Forward Jonathan David dribbles during a 2024 Copa América match.

Midfielder Diana Matheson is on the attack during a 2014 match.

Midfielder Diana Matheson was one of Canada's longest-serving players. She appeared in more than 200 games for the team. She scored key goals, including a game winner against France in the 2012 Olympics.

SHE SHOOTS, SHE SCORES!

Christine Sinclair played and scored in five different World Cups. She is one of only three players ever to do that. The others are Brazilian star Marta and Portugal's Cristiano Ronaldo.

No player in the world scored more international goals than Christine Sinclair. She played for Canada's women's team from 2000 to 2023. She scored more than 190 goals. Many fans call her the greatest Canadian soccer player of all time.

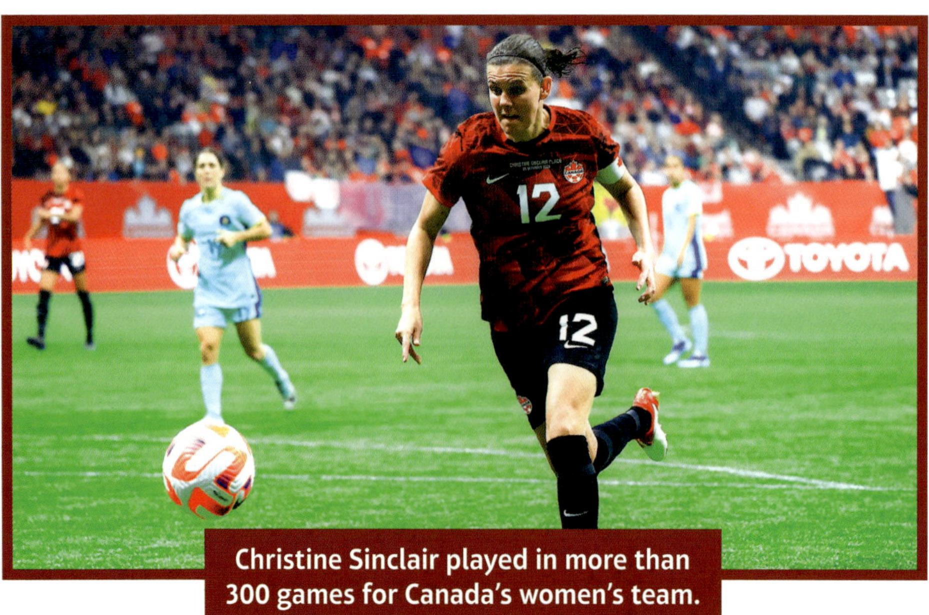

Christine Sinclair played in more than 300 games for Canada's women's team.

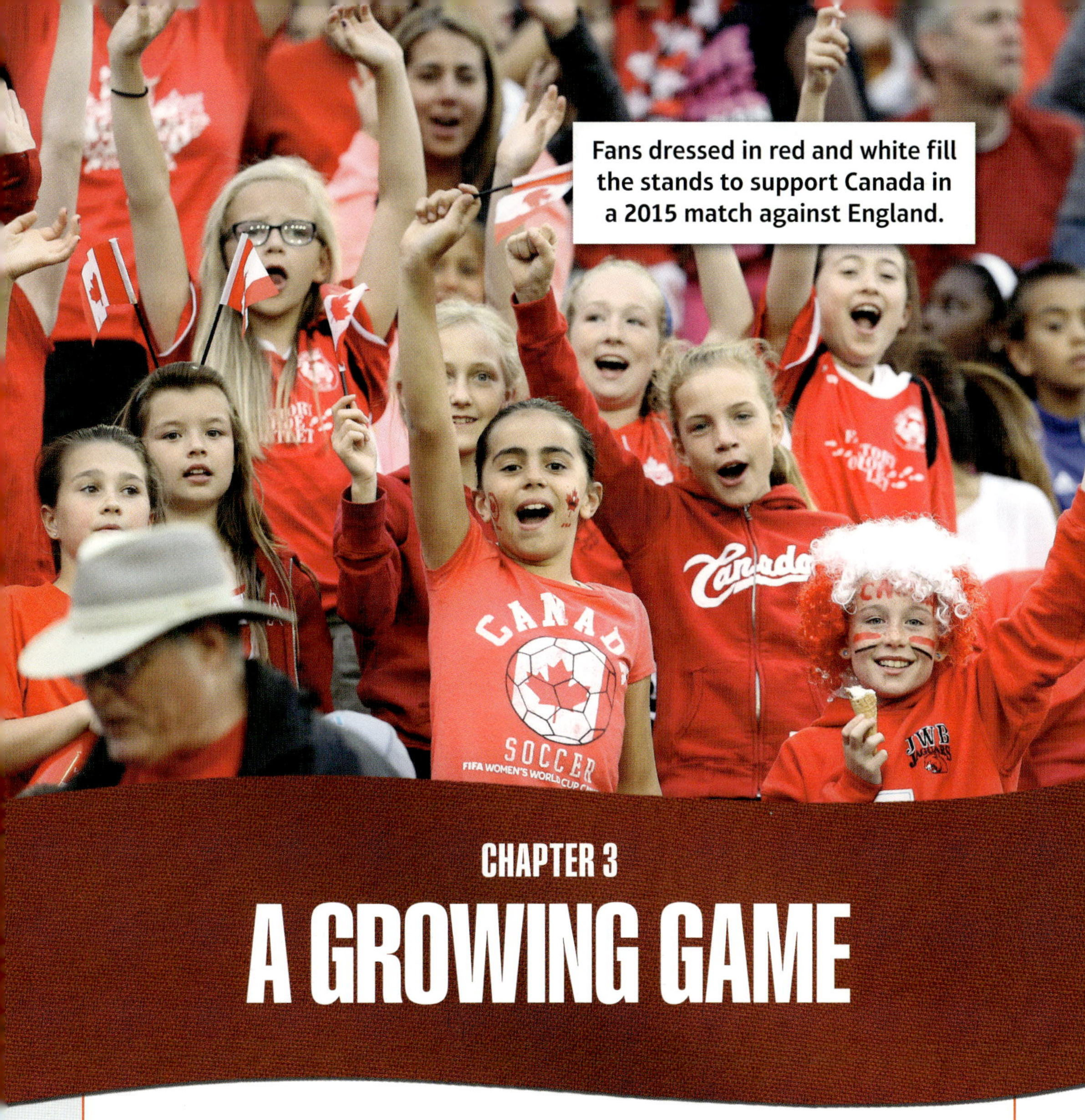

Fans dressed in red and white fill the stands to support Canada in a 2015 match against England.

CHAPTER 3

A GROWING GAME

Canada is known for its cold weather but also for the fiery passion of its sports fans. Crowds across the country are cheering for their teams and helping soccer grow. From increased supporters to new leagues and big dreams for the future, Canadian soccer is on the rise.

In the early days, Canadian soccer didn't have an organized group of fans as other countries do. But in 1996, a group of passionate supporters called the Voyageurs formed. They wanted to bring energy and excitement to Canadian soccer games.

The Voyageurs travel to matches, wave Canadian flags, bang on drums, and sing loud songs to support Canada's teams. Whether it's the men's team, the women's team, or club teams, they are always there, making noise and showing their love for Canadian soccer. Their passion has helped grow the sport and inspire new generations of fans.

Canadian fans celebrate a goal at a 2024 match.

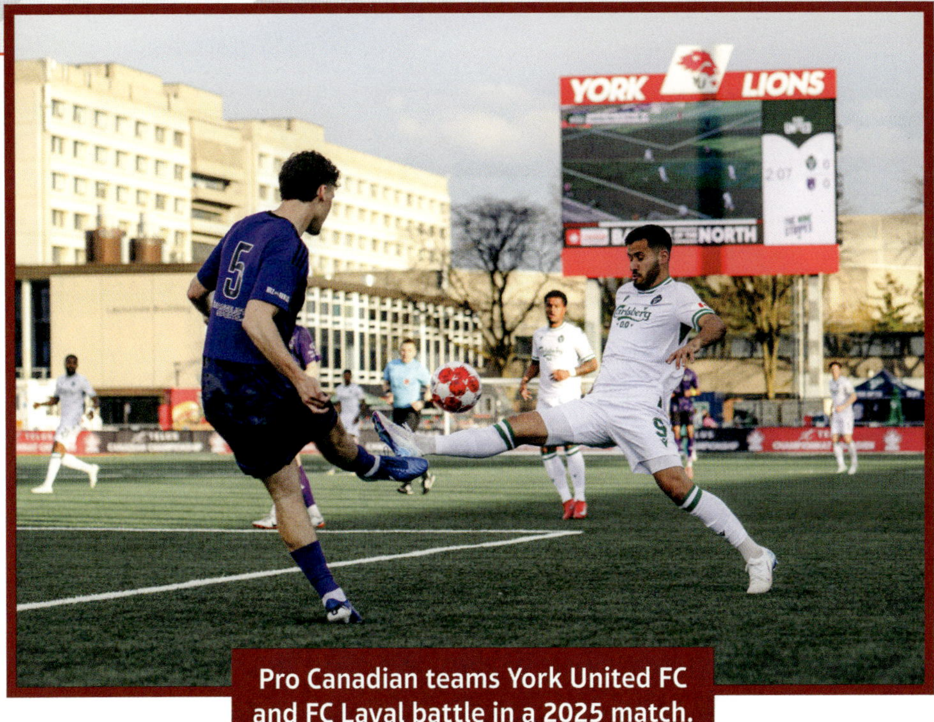

Pro Canadian teams York United FC and FC Laval battle in a 2025 match.

For a long time, Canada didn't have its own pro soccer league. But in 2019, the Canadian Premier League (CPL) launched. This new league gave Canadian men's players a chance to develop their skills and play in front of local fans.

BON VOYAGEUR!

Canadian soccer fans are called Voyageurs in honor of the French-Canadian fur traders who voyaged across Canada, often by canoe.

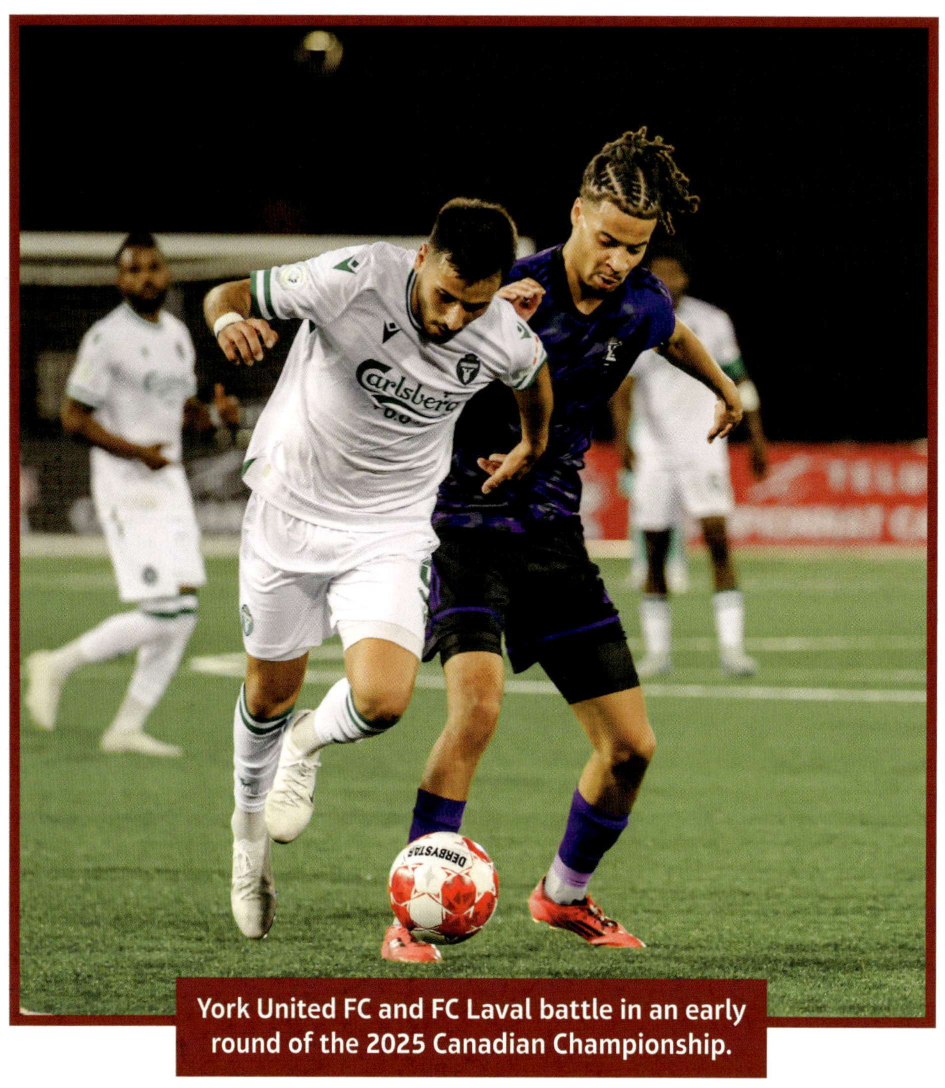

York United FC and FC Laval battle in an early round of the 2025 Canadian Championship.

The CPL has teams across the country, from Halifax, Nova Scotia, to Vancouver Island, British Columbia. It helps young players improve and gives soccer fans a league to call their own. As the CPL continues to grow, it will help Canada become even stronger in the global game.

The 2026 World Cup will be special for Canada. The country is cohosting the men's tournament along with the United States and Mexico. This means some of the biggest soccer matches in the world will be played on Canadian soil.

Canada's men's team is getting ready for this huge event. After qualifying for the 2022 World Cup, they now have bigger goals—to win the World Cup in 2026. With stars like Alphonso Davies and Jonathan David, the team is full of talent. Fans are excited to see how far Canada can go.

Fans proudly display the Canadian flag while supporting Toronto FC in a 2025 professional match.

The Northern Super League launched in 2025. It gives the top Canadian women a chance to compete at the pro level.

Canada's women's team is already one of the best in the world, but there is still more work to do. Many fans and players believed Canada needed a women's pro league to help develop future stars. In 2025, that became a reality.

The Northern Super League (NSL), Canada's first pro women's soccer league, launched in April 2025. The NSL is made up of six founding clubs from across Canada: Vancouver, Calgary, Toronto, Ottawa, Montreal, and Halifax. The league aims to elevate women's soccer in Canada and provide new opportunities for players.

Canadian soccer is growing faster than ever. With new leagues and strong national teams, the future looks bright. Wherever the teams go, the Voyageurs will be there chanting, banging drums, and cheering them on.

AFC Toronto and Montreal Roses FC battle in an April 2025 NSL match.

CANADA MEN'S SOCCER TIMELINE

1924 Canada plays its first official international match.

1985 Canada wins its first CONCACAF Championship, qualifying for the 1986 World Cup.

1986 Canada makes its World Cup debut.

2000 The team wins the CONCACAF Gold Cup, qualifying for the 2001 Confederations Cup.

2022 Canada qualifies for its second World Cup.

2023 Canada finishes as runners-up in the CONCACAF Nations League Finals.

2024 The team competes in its first Copa América, finishing fourth.

2026 Canada is set to cohost the World Cup alongside the United States and Mexico.

CANADA WOMEN'S SOCCER TIMELINE

1986 Canada plays its first official international match, defeating the United States 2–1.

1991 Canada competes in the first CONCACAF Women's Championship, finishing second.

1995 The team participates in its first Women's World Cup.

2008 Canada makes its Olympic debut at the Summer Olympics in Beijing, China.

2012 The team wins the bronze medal at the Olympics in London, England.

2016 Canada earns bronze at the Rio de Janeiro, Brazil, Olympics.

2021 Canada wins gold at the Tokyo Olympics.

2024 The team qualifies for its fifth consecutive Olympic Games, defeating Jamaica in a playoff.

GLOSSARY

club team: an amateur or pro team that is not a national team

CONCACAF: a group that oversees soccer in North American, Central American, and Caribbean nations

extra time: time added to the end of a tied game

goalkeeper: the player who stands in front of the goal and tries to stop the other team from scoring

immigrant: a person who moves permanently to another country

midfielder: a player whose main jobs are to pass the ball and defend

penalty kick: a free shot at the goal after a foul or to decide some games

qualifying match: a game that teams play to earn their way into a tournament

refugee: a person who flees to a foreign country to escape danger and seek safety

shoot-out: a shooting contest used to determine the winner of a tied game

LEARN MORE

Canada Soccer
https://canadasoccer.com/

Kiddle: Football Facts for Kids
https://kids.kiddle.co/Football

Scheff, Matt. *The World Cup: Soccer's Greatest Tournament*. Lerner Publications, 2021.

Science Kids: Fun Soccer Facts for Kids
https://www.sciencekids.co.nz/sciencefacts/sports/soccer.html

Shaw, Gina. *What Is the Women's World Cup?* Penguin Workshop, 2023.

Streeter, Anthony. *World Cup All-Time Greats*. Press Box, 2025.

INDEX

PHOTO ACKNOWLEDGMENTS

Image credits: Naomi Baker/Getty Images, pp. 4, 7; Brad Smith/ISI Photos/Getty Images, p. 6; GEORGES GOBET/AFP via Getty Images, p. 8; Bob Thomas/Popperfoto via Getty Images, p. 9; Mike King/Allsport/Hulton Archive/Getty Images, p. 10; Eric Verhoeven/Soccrates/Getty Images, p. 11; MIGUEL MEDINA/AFP/Getty Images, p. 12; LOIC VENANCE/AFP via Getty Images, p. 13; Dale MacMillan/Soccrates/Getty Images, pp. 14–16; Steve Russell/Toronto Star via Getty Images, p. 17; Stephen Nadler/ISI Photos/Getty Images, p. 18; Derek Leung/Getty Images, p. 19; Indrawan Kumala/NurPhoto via Getty Images, pp. 20, 22; Vaughn Ridley/PA Images/Alamy, p. 21; Curtis Wong/SPP/Sipa via AP Images, pp. 23–24; Anatoliy Cherkasov/Informa Plus Photo Agency/LightRocket via Getty Image, p. 25; Nick Lachance/Toronto Star via Getty Images, pp. 26–27. Design elements: Ralf Hiemisch/Getty Images; Rifqyhsn Design/Getty Images; cunfek/Getty Images; poo worawit/Getty Images.

Cover images: Amy Elle/SPP/Sipa via AP Images (left); AP Photo/Tony Gutierre (right).